Four are the seasons
I know them all
Spring, summer,
winter and fall

One Is a Drummer

A BOOK OF NUMBERS

written by Roseanne Thong  illustrated by Grace Lin

McGraw Hill Education

One is a drummer
 One is a race
One is a dragon boat
 that wins first place!

One is a tail
   and a cool, wet nose
One is a tongue
   that tickles my toes

Two are the greetings
on our wall
"Luck" and "Fortune"
for us all

Three are the steamers
Three are the buns
Three are the egg tarts—
here they come!

There are so many numbers
at home and at play
How many have
you counted today?

Dragon Boat Festival: During this celebration, people remember the famous poet Qu Yuan who died long ago. He is said to have leaped into a river when an evil king captured his kingdom. Fishermen tried to save Qu Yuan by beating on drums and splashing their oars to keep the water dragons away. When they realized it was too late, they scattered rice dumplings into the river so that his soul would never be hungry. A special kind of rice dumpling called *zhong-zi* is eaten to remember Qu Yuan. It is made of glutinous rice and wrapped in bamboo leaves.

Dragon Boats: Complete with ferocious heads, scales and long, thin bodies, these boats are raced during the Dragon Boat Festival. A drummer sits up front and beats out the pace, as rowers follow with their oars.

New Year Greetings: At the New Year, bright red banners carrying wishes for luck, good fortune and new beginnings are hung on the walls and doors of homes, restaurants and public places.

Dim Sum: A Cantonese term meaning "a little heart," dim sum refers to little snacks or treats that are eaten with Chinese tea for breakfast or lunch. They are often served three at a time in bamboo steamers. Some popular dim sum items include shrimp dumplings, barbecued pork buns, meatballs and egg tarts.

Mahjong: This traditional Chinese game requires four players and uses 144 rectangular tiles made of plastic or wood. The tiles come in suits of bamboo, dots, numbers, winds, flowers, dragons and directions (north, south, east, west), and make a delightful clicking noise when they are laid on the table.

Eight Immortals: These legendary beings are based on real people who lived long ago. The immortals carry Taoist symbols: a basket of flowers, a sword, castanets, a fan, a gourd, a flute, a tube drum and a lotus blossom.

Bamboo: This plant is favored by Chinese in home and temple gardens. There is a saying that people should try to grow up straight and strong, just like bamboo.

Roseanne Thong was born in Southern California, but now lives in Hong Kong with her husband and daughter where she writes and teaches English. The Dragon Boat Festival is one of her favorite holidays. To learn about dragon boats and other Chinese traditions, visit her Web site at www.greenfield-thong.com.

Grace Lin attended the Rhode Island School of Design for **four** years. She has published **three** books with Chronicle. She has **two** sisters and **one** husband. She also has **one** Web site: www.gracelin.com. She hopes more than **ten** readers will visit her there.

To my good friend Irene, who advised me to "just do it!" —R. T.
To Karma Lilian Kendall, who is niece number one —G. L.

mhreadingwonders.com

Text ©2014 by Roseanne Greenfield Thong.
Illustrations ©2014 by Grace Lin.
Use by permission of Chronicle Books.

No part of this publication may be reproduced
or distributed in any form or by an means,
or stored in a database or retrieval system, without the
prior written consent of McGraw-Hill Education,
including, but not limited to, network storage or
transmission, or broadcast for distance learning.

Send all inquiries to:
McGraw-Hill Education
Two Penn Plaza
New York NY 10121

ISBN: 978-0-07-678365-6
MHID: 0-07-678365-0

Printed in Mexico

9 BRP 25

Six are the horses
on a merry-go-round
Six are the children
going up and down!

Eight are the napkins
Eight are the dishes
Eight are the candles
for making wishes

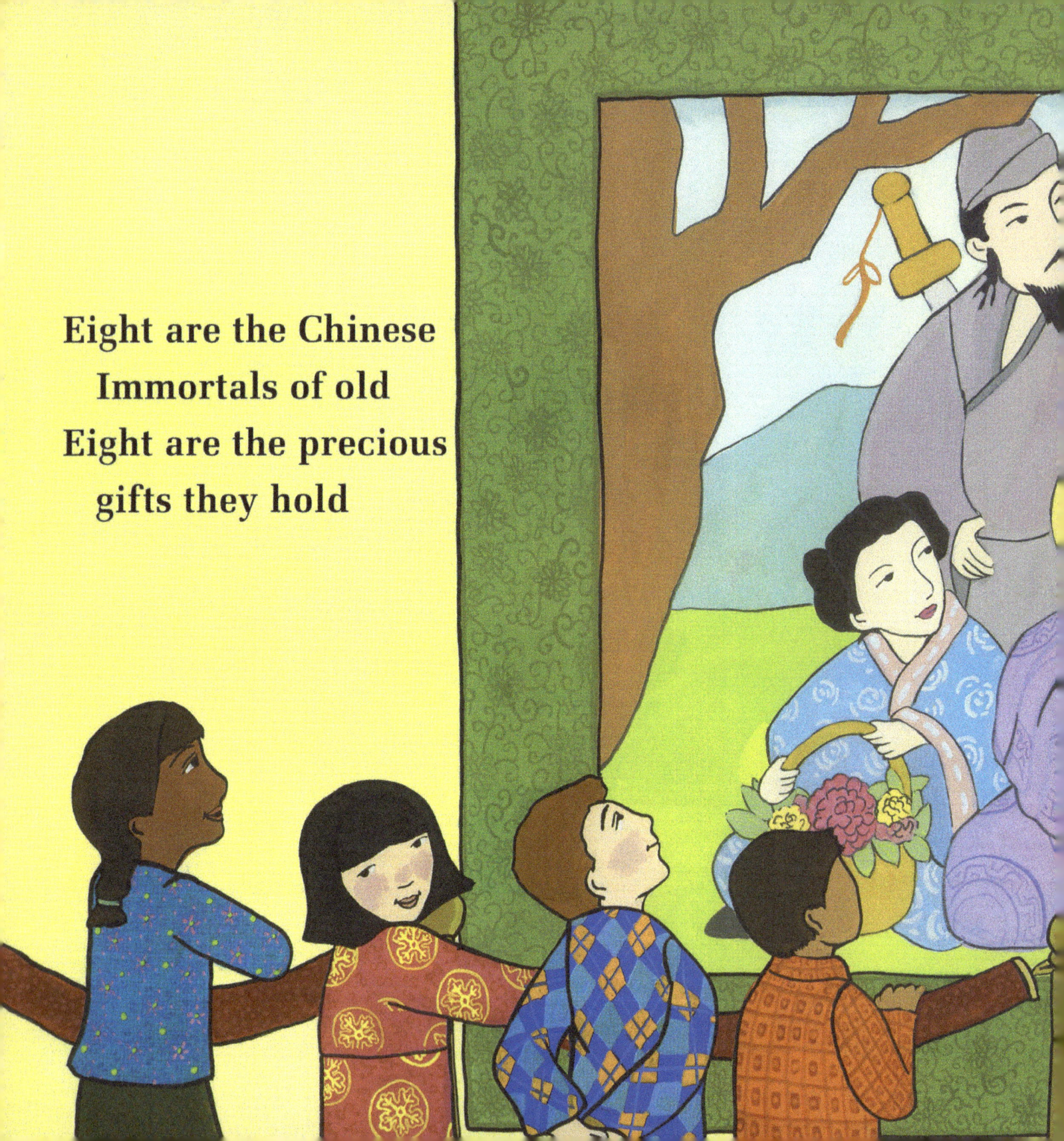

Eight are the Chinese Immortals of old
Eight are the precious gifts they hold